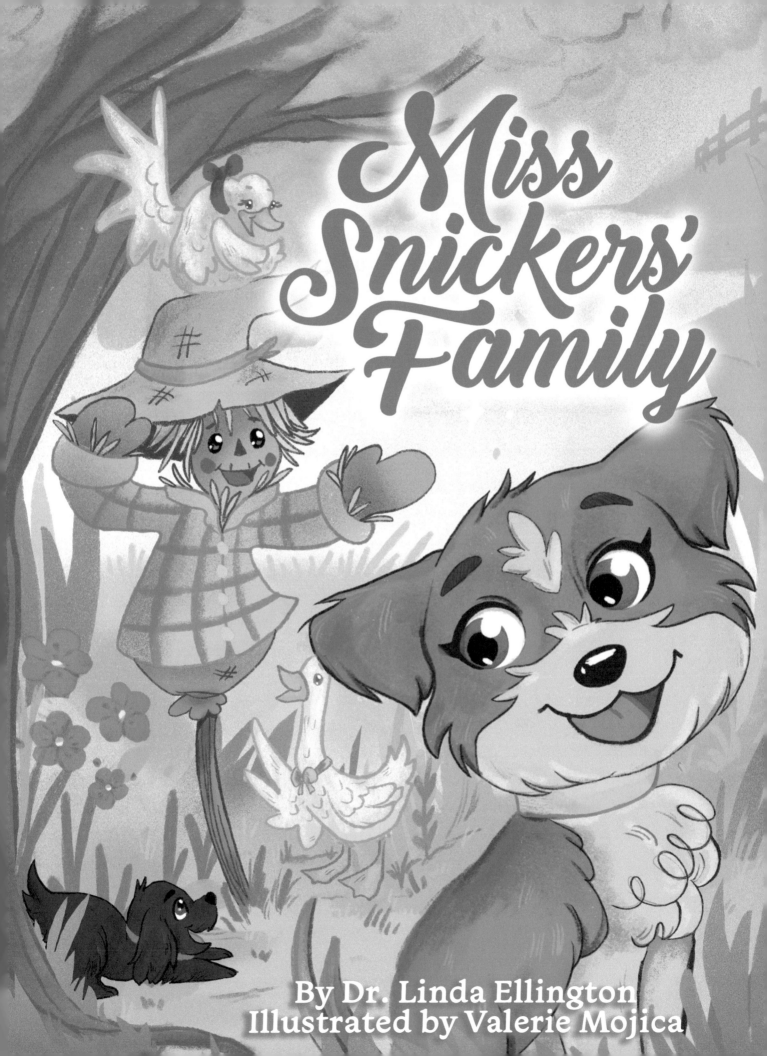

Miss Snickers' Family

By Dr. Linda Ellington

Illustrated by Valerie Mojica

Archway Publishing books may be ordered through booksellers or by contacting:

Archway Publishing
1663 Liberty Drive
Bloomington, IN 47403
www.archwaypublishing.com
844-669-3957

Because of the dynamic nature of the Internet, any web addresses or links contained in this book may have changed since publication and may no longer be valid. The views expressed in this work are solely those of the author and do not necessarily reflect the views of the publisher, and the publisher hereby disclaims any responsibility for them.

ISBN: 978-1-6657-3914-6 (sc)
ISBN: 978-1-6657-3915-3 (hc)
ISBN: 978-1-6657-3913-9 (e)

Print information available on the last page.

Archway Publishing rev. date: 02/27/2023

ARCHWAY
PUBLISHING

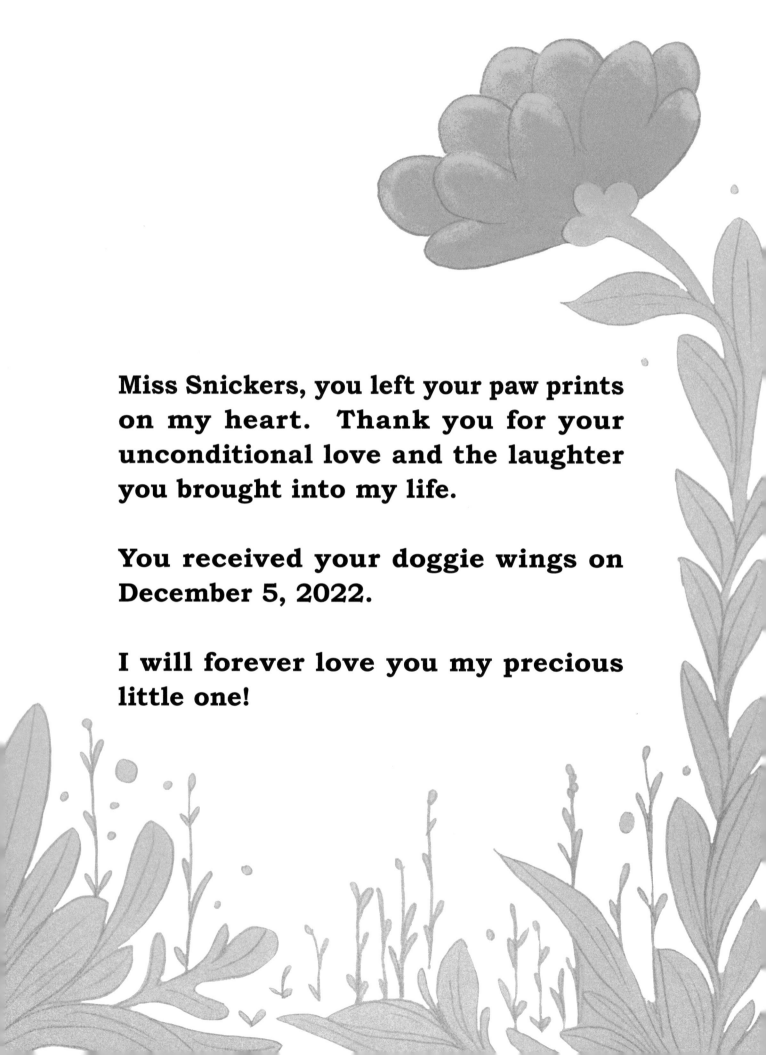

Miss Snickers, you left your paw prints on my heart. Thank you for your unconditional love and the laughter you brought into my life.

You received your doggie wings on December 5, 2022.

I will forever love you my precious little one!

Woof Woof . . .

Hello everyone, my name is Miss Snickers and I am excited to have my family say hi to all of you.

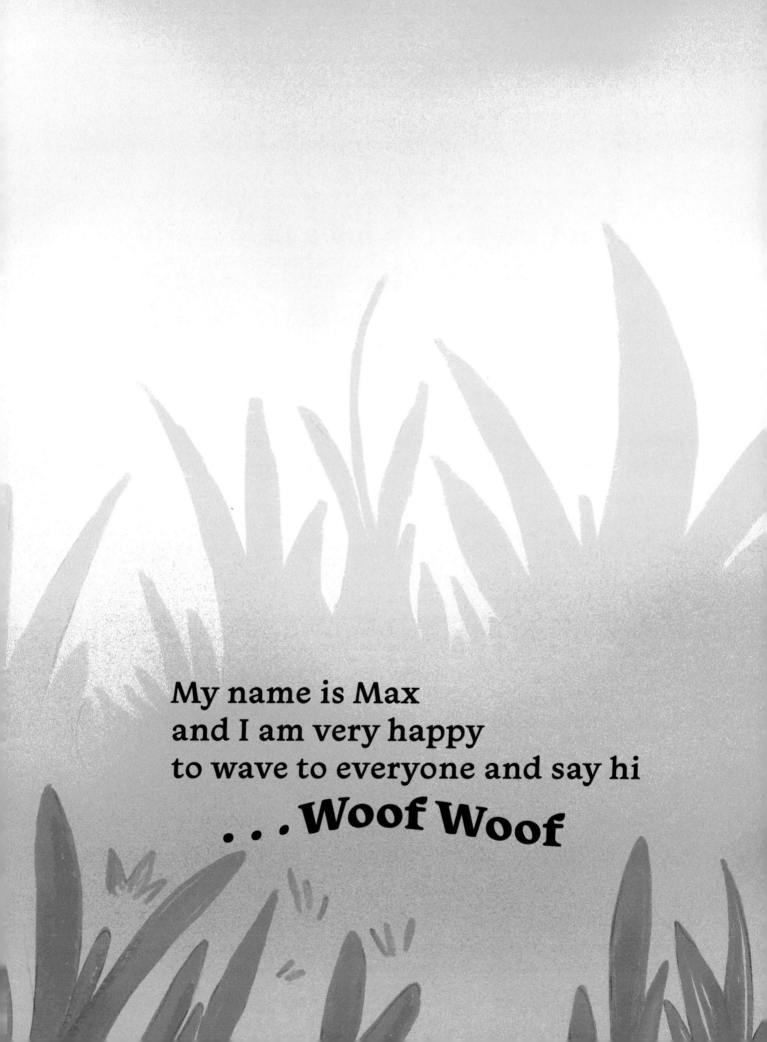

My name is Max
and I am very happy
to wave to everyone and say hi
. . . Woof Woof

My name is Guss and I am a geese.

Honk **Honk** . . . Hello

My name is Gabbie and I also am a Geese **Honk Honk** . . . Hi

I am Hattie, a scarecrow in the family.

Caw...Caw...

that is me saying Hello.

Snickers says,
       "I am so happy! "

Max asks Snickers,
"why are you happy?"

Snickers says I'm lucky.

I have a family that is all of you. Wow!

Gus and Gabbie look puzzled
at Miss Snickers and ask
if it is ok to be different
but in the same family?

Yes!

There are many different types of families.

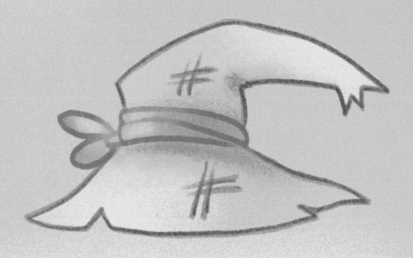

Hattie says even a scarecrow
like me can be in a family.

Max says loving and taking care of each other is what really makes a family.

Gus and Gabbie laugh and say, we are a family and we look alike and different.

Hattie also laughs and says
"hey look at me I am different too."

Miss Snickers smiles and says
"see all of us are lucky — we are a family
who will stick together with love!"

Hattie says
"ok family let us go
together to play!"

Max says
"Can we eat too I am hungry!"

Printed in the United States
by Baker & Taylor Publisher Services